GREEK MYTHOLOGY

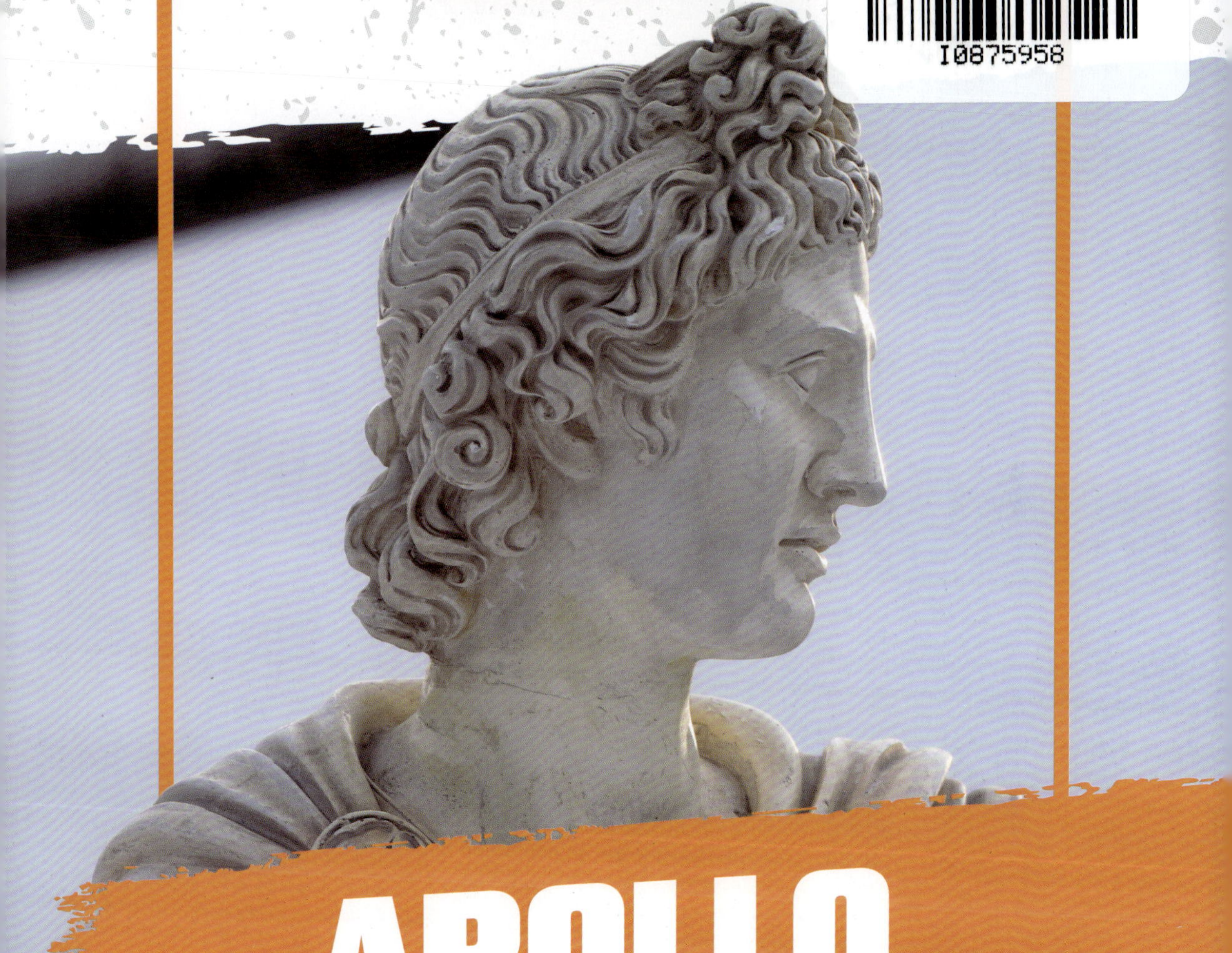

APOLLO,

God of Art and Healing

BY JOANNA BLAIR

Enslow PUBLISHING

Please visit our website, www.enslow.com. For a free color catalog of all our high-quality books, call toll free 1-800-398-2504 or fax 1-877-980-4454.

Cataloging-in-Publication Data
Names: Blair, Joanna.
Title: Apollo, god of art and healing / Joanna Blair.
Description: Buffalo, NY : Enslow Publishing, 2027. | Series: Greek mythology | Includes glossary and index.
Identifiers: ISBN 9781978550803 (pbk.) | ISBN 9781978550810 (library bound) | ISBN 9781978550827 (ebook)
Subjects: LCSH: Apollo (Deity)--Juvenile literature. | Gods, Greek--Juvenile literature. | Mythology, Greek--Juvenile literature.
Classification: LCC BL820.A7 B535 2027 | DDC 292.2113--dc23

Published in 2027 by
Enslow Publishing
2544 Clinton Street
Buffalo, NY 14224

Portions of this work were originally authored by Christine Ha and published as *Apollo*. All new material in this edition was authored by Joanna Blair.

Cover Designer: Joshua Olson
Interior Designer: Joshua Olson
Editor: Claire Vanden Branden

Photo Credits: Cover, p. 1 Peyker/Shutterstock.com; pp. 4–5, 8–9 Gilmanshin/Shutterstock.com; pp. 6–7 Roberto Caucino/Shutterstock.com"; pp. 10–11 Rawpixel.com/Shutterstock.com; p. 12 Vladimir Korostyshevskiy/Shutterstock.com; p. 13 Brittany Graham LA/Shutterstock.com; pp. 14–15 Storm Is Me/Shutterstock.com; pp. 16–17 Milan_PE/Shutterstock.com; pp. 18, 29 delcarmat/Shutterstock.com; p. 19 Angel Simon/Shutterstock.com; p. 20 Zwiebackesser/Shutterstock.com; p. 21 b113/Shutterstock.com; pp. 22–23 Leon Rafael/Shutterstock.com; pp. 24–25 Jethro T./Shutterstock.com; p. 26 Zina Seletskaya/Shutterstock.com; pp. 26–27 Boris Stroujko/Shutterstock.com.

Printed in China

CPSIA compliance information: Batch #QS27ENS: For further information contact Enslow Publishing, at 1-800-398-2504.

TABLE OF CONTENTS

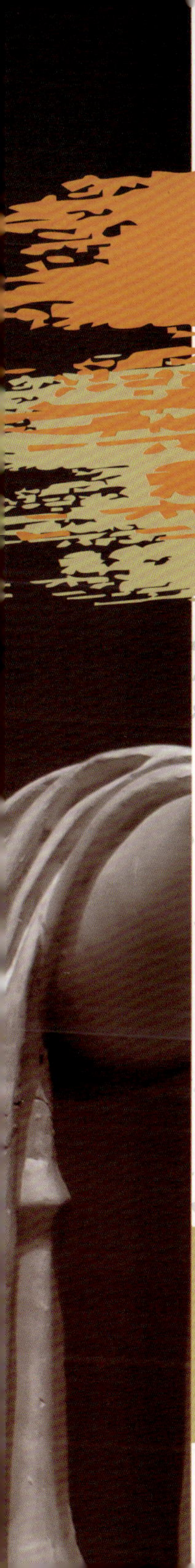

CHAPTER 1

AN IMPORTANT GOD

Apollo was one of the 12 main Greek gods. He had power over many things. They included art, music, **prophecy**, medicine, and **archery**.

Apollo was one of the few gods who had the same name in both Greek and Roman myths.

Apollo helped people make music and art. He appears in many paintings.

Apollo was a god of justice, law, and order. He helped people have peace and safety. He also watched over governments and cities.

Apollo was a skilled archer. His arrows never missed their targets.

Apollo got his lyre from the god Hermes.

Apollo played a **lyre**. This instrument made beautiful music. It also had magical powers. It could **charm** people.

PROUD MUSICIAN

Once, Apollo and the god Pan had a music contest. Apollo won. But one listener thought Pan was better. Apollo got angry. He cursed that man by giving him donkey ears.

CHAPTER 2

FAMOUS MYTHS

The Greeks told many **myths** about Apollo. In one, he killed a giant snake. He shot it with his arrows.

In some versions of the story, the monster Apollo defeated was a dragon instead of a snake.

Every day, Apollo rode a **chariot** across the sky. It was pulled by fiery horses. They brought light to the world.

A carving of Apollo's chariot can be found on a theater in Milan, Italy.

The goddess Artemis protected girls and young women.

APOLLO'S TWIN

Apollo had a twin sister named Artemis. She was the goddess of the moon and hunting. She rode her own chariot across the sky. It brought night.

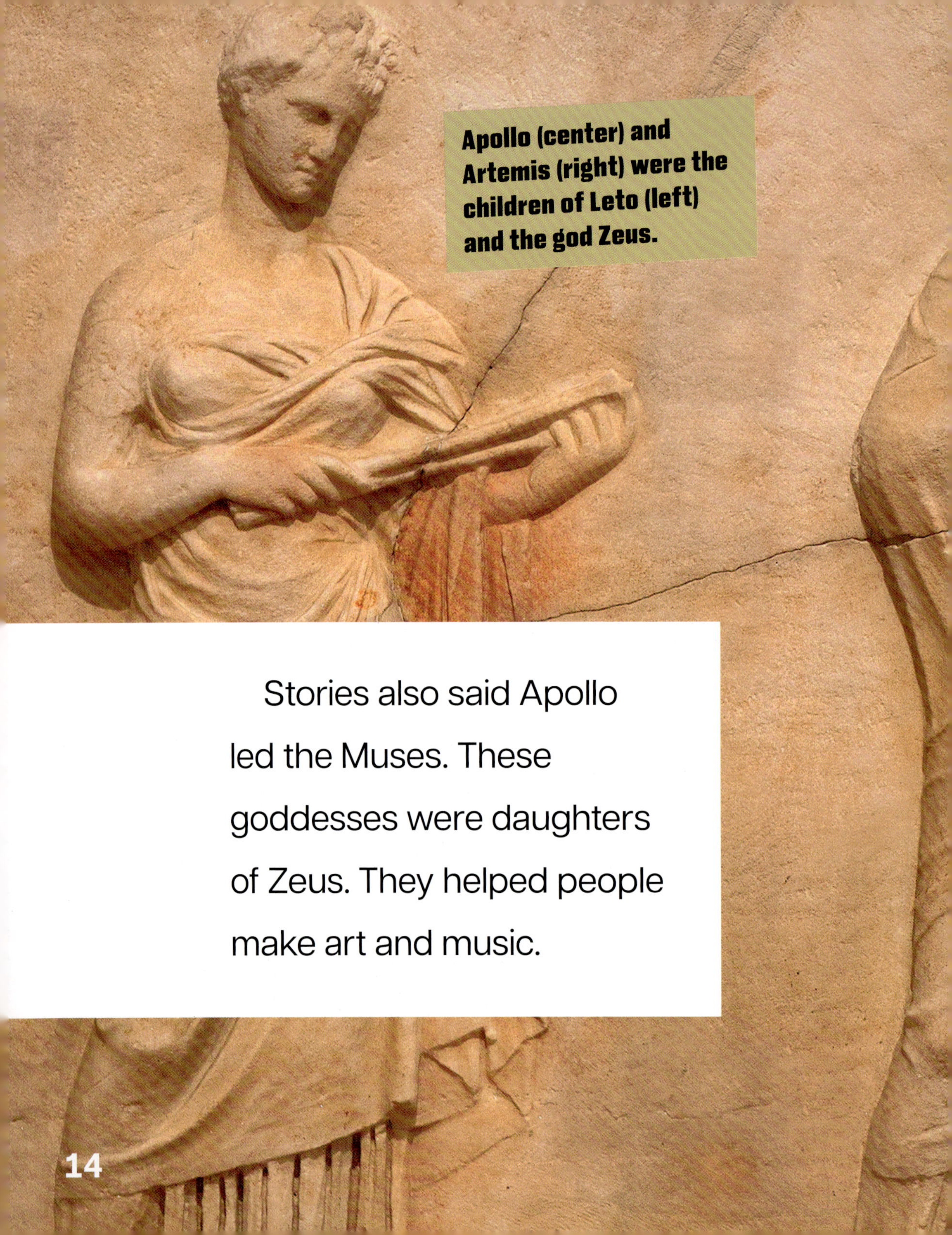

Apollo (center) and Artemis (right) were the children of Leto (left) and the god Zeus.

Stories also said Apollo led the Muses. These goddesses were daughters of Zeus. They helped people make art and music.

In early Greek stories, Helios was the god of the sun. But people combined Helios and Apollo into one figure over time.

CHAPTER 3

BAD AT ROMANCE

Apollo was described as young and handsome. He fell in love often. But it usually ended badly. Many of his lovers died suddenly.

Apollo once loved a prince from Sparta. Legends say blue flowers grew where the prince died.

The god Eros made Apollo (right) fall in love with Daphne (left). Then he made Daphne run from Apollo.

Apollo loved Daphne. She was turned into a laurel tree. Its leaves became a **symbol** of Apollo.

Other people didn't love Apollo back. He did not like being rejected. He sometimes punished these people.

Apollo is often shown wearing a crown of laurel leaves.

For example, Apollo loved Cassandra. He taught her prophecy. But she did not want to be with him. He was angry. So, he made it so that no one believed what she **predicted**.

Cassandra predicted that the city of Troy would fall. But people ignored her warnings.

Apollo sometimes used crows to send messages or spy on people.

WHY CROWS ARE BLACK

Apollo once loved a woman named Coronis. A white crow told Apollo that Coronis was not loyal to him. Apollo became angry. He burned the crow's feathers. They turned black.

CHAPTER 4

MANY TEMPLES

The Greeks built many temples for Apollo. The most important temple was in the city of Delphi. This temple had a famous **oracle**.

Ruins of the Temple of Apollo at Delphi still stand today.

A treasury building held the gifts people brought to the Temple of Apollo at Delphi.

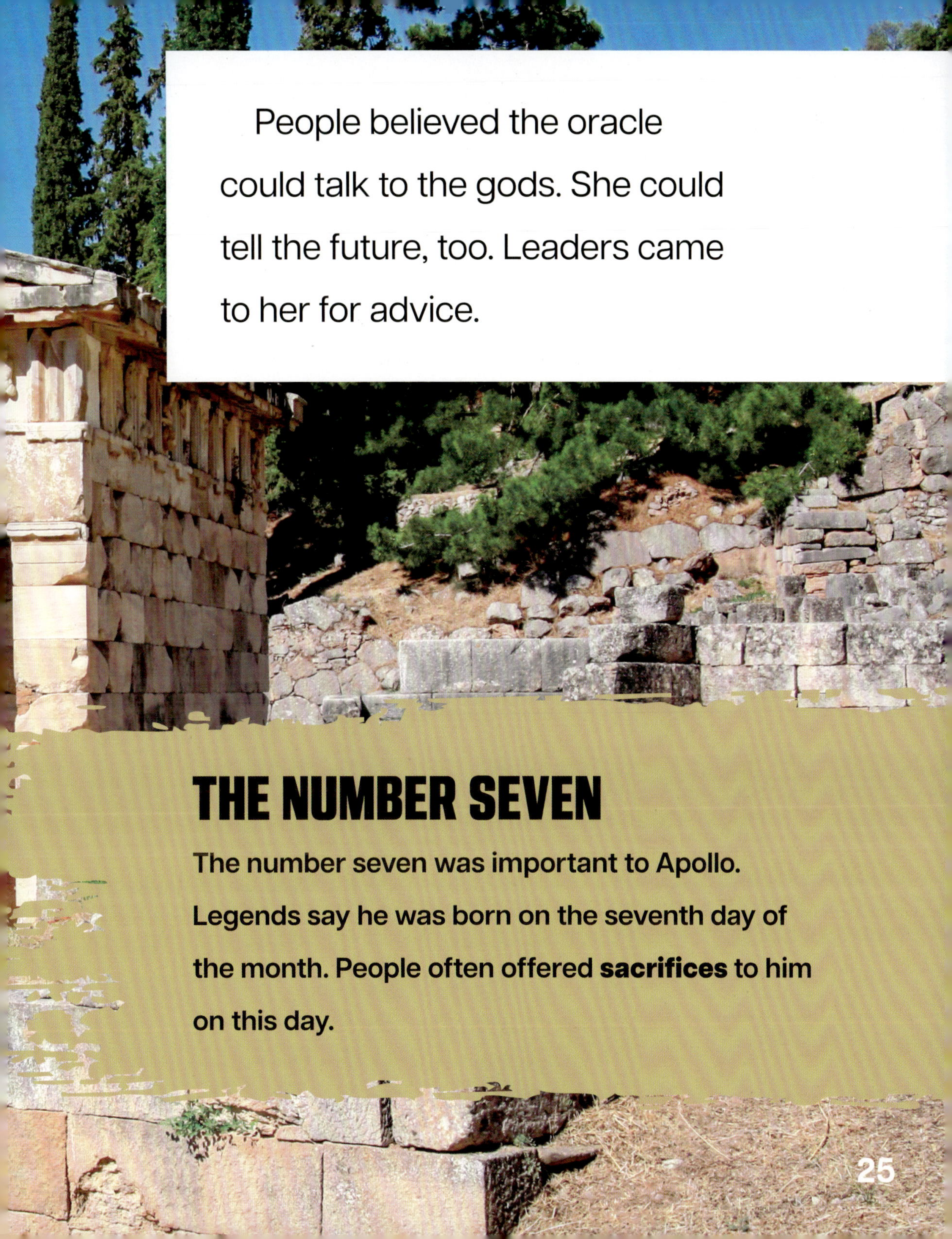

People believed the oracle could talk to the gods. She could tell the future, too. Leaders came to her for advice.

THE NUMBER SEVEN

The number seven was important to Apollo. Legends say he was born on the seventh day of the month. People often offered **sacrifices** to him on this day.

The temple stood on a mountain. It was hard to get to. But people came from all over. They brought laurel branches, money, and sacrifices. In return, they got advice.

A holy stone at Delphi was said to mark the center of the world.

A statue of Apollo guards the ruins of a temple in Italy.

Apollo had temples outside Greece, too. Some were as far away as Egypt and Turkey.

TEST YOUR KNOWLEDGE

Take this quiz to test your knowledge.

1. Write a few sentences explaining the main ideas of Chapter 3.
2. Would you want to have someone predict your future? Why or why not?
3. Where was the most important temple of Apollo located?
   - A. Egypt
   - B. Delphi
   - C. Turkey
4. Why would people bring laurel branches to Apollo's temple?
   - A. Laurel trees were very expensive.
   - B. Laurel trees were not important.
   - C. Laurel trees were a symbol of Apollo.

5. What does **cursed** mean in this book?

Apollo got angry. He ***cursed*** *that man by giving him donkey ears.*

A. made friends with someone
B. hurt someone with magic
C. was kind to someone

6. What does **rejected** mean in this book?

Other people didn't love him back. Apollo did not like being ***rejected****.*

A. prayed to
B. followed around
C. not loved or wanted

Answers can be found on page 32.

GLOSSARY

archery
The skill of shooting arrows with a bow.

chariot
A two-wheeled cart pulled by horses or other animals.

charm
To use magic to control someone or something.

lyre
A stringed instrument that is similar to a small harp.

myths
Well-known stories from the past that often include magic.

oracle
A person who tells messages to and from the gods.

predicted
Said that something will happen in the future.

prophecy
The ability to predict the future.

sacrifices
Gifts to gods or goddesses to win their help or favor.

symbol
An object or idea that stands for and reminds people of something else.

FOR MORE INFORMATION

BOOKS

Curtis, Kenny and Jillian Hughes. *Greeking Out: Heroes and Olympians.* Washington, DC: National Geographic, 2024.

Tracosas, L. J. *Ultimate Greek Mythology.* New York, NY: Penguin Random House, 2023.

WEBSITES

Britannica Kids: Apollo

kids.britannica.com/kids/article/Apollo/352767

Read more myths about Apollo at this website.

National Geographic Kids: The Gods and Goddesses of Ancient Greece!

natgeokids.com/nz/discover/history/greece/greek-gods

Learn more about Greek gods and goddesses.

Publisher's note to educators and parents: Our editors have carefully reviewed these websites to ensure that they are suitable for students. Many websites change frequently, however, and we cannot guarantee that a site's future contents will continue to meet our high standards of quality and educational value. Be advised that students should be closely supervised whenever they access the internet.

INDEX

Answer Key:
1. Answers will vary; 2. Answers will vary; 3. B; 4. C; 5. B; 6. C